TA

Unless otherwise indicated, all Scripture quotations are taken from the King James Version of the Bible.
How To Turn Your Mistakes Into Miracles
Wisdom Key Books · ISBN 1-56394-041-8/B-56
Copyright © 1997 by **MIKE MURDOCK**
All publishing rights belong exclusively to Wisdom International
Publisher/Editor: Deborah Murdock Johnson
Published by The Wisdom Center
4051 Denton Hwy · Ft Worth, Texas 76117
1-888-WISDOM-1 (1-888-947-3661)
Website: thewisdomcenter.tv

WHY I WROTE THIS BOOK

Mistakes Happen.

This Is A Human World. You will find that mistakes are just a part of your daily life. Mistakes happen on the *job,* in your *choice* of friends and even in *financial decisions.*

Though some mistakes can be devastating, the majority of your mistakes can be turned around for your good!

Yesterday's failure can become *today's* success. *Tragedies* can become *triumphs.*

You can change the direction of your life! *YOU can step OUT* of failure into a victorious and successful life. Your CREATOR and Heavenly Father has anticipated your problems and has laid out a PLAN for turning your mistakes into miracles!!

Your Greatest Mistake Can Become The Golden Bridge To Your Success.

That is why I wrote this book.

Mike Murdock

What You Fail To Master
In Your Life
Will Eventually
Master You.

-MIKE MURDOCK

✑ **1** ✑
ACCEPT YOUR HUMANITY

You Are Not God.

Neither do you have "angel wings." Your possibilities of making a mistake are one hundred percent. Your response to your mistakes determines your success.

God anticipated your weaknesses. "Like as a father pitieth his children, so the Lord pitieth them that fear Him. For He knoweth our frame; He remembereth that we *are* dust" (Psalm 103:13,14).

True, some use the flimsy comment, "I'm just human," as a "cop-out" and cover-up instead of a motivation for higher principles. But thousands who learn to *accept* themselves as human beings learn to enjoy life so much better.

Avoid deadly self-criticism.

Accept your humanity as the birthplace for pursuing God and His Divine nature being formed in you.

Nothing Is Ever
As Bad As
It First Appears.

-MIKE MURDOCK

≈ 2 ≈
ADMIT YOUR MISTAKE

Confession Often Silences Accusers.

You Cannot Correct What You Are Unwilling To Confront.

1. Recognize And Admit Any Mistake... Yourself. Do not justify it. Do not lie to yourself. The Scriptures say: "He that covereth his sins shall not prosper: but whoso confesseth and forsaketh *them* shall have mercy" (Proverbs 28:13).

2. Confess Your Mistake To God. "If we confess our sins, He is faithful and just to forgive us our sins, and to cleanse us from all unrighteousness" (1 John 1:9).

3. Confess The Mistake To Others Who Were Damaged By Your Mistake. "And when ye stand praying, forgive, if ye have ought against any: that your Father also which is in heaven may forgive you your trespasses" (Mark 11:25).

4. Do Not Confess Your Mistakes To Anyone Desiring To Use It As A Weapon To Destroy You Or Others. *When your confession would destroy a marriage or home, confess to God alone.* "In the multitude of words there wanteth not sin: but he that refraineth his lips is wise" (Proverbs 10:19).

5. Express Your Plan For Restitution And Compensation To Those Who Experienced Losses Through Your Mistake. Who have you damaged? Whose life or income did your mistake hurt? Present your plan for restoring what you have taken. The Zacchaeus Principle is very important. Return four times what you have taken.

The Proof Of Repentance Is Restitution.

❧ **3** ❧

ASSIGN THE RESPONSIBILITY OF THE MISTAKE TO THOSE TRULY RESPONSIBLE

The Guilty Must Pay.

If others are involved, you must allow them to accept their own share of the blame.

Assuming all responsibility for *others* opens the door to bitterness, resentment and self-pity. Besides, you actually *add* to their own success by forcing them to *account* for themselves. Parents who always "cover" for little Johnny or Susie destroy their children's opportunity to embrace *responsibility.* "Chasten thy son while there is hope, and let not thy soul spare for his crying" (Proverbs 19:18).

"I've got to go get my husband out of the bar tonight. He's drinking again," a heartbroken lovely lady told me one night.

I replied, "Why?"

She looked surprised. "Well...uh ...he...uh."

I said, "If you keep cushioning the fall, he'll never quit jumping. *You've got to let him hit the bottom.* Then, and only then, will he want to reach for the top."

Pain Decides Change. Until The Guilty feels *loss,* they will *never* change.

Learn from the prodigal son.

The *tears* of his father did not affect him.

The *goodness* of his father did not activate him to return.

The stench of *the pig pen* birthed the *desire* for change.

God uses two basic motivators in your life: People and Pain.

Don't Stop The Divine Cycle.

≈ 4 ≈

REVIEW THE OPTIONS AVAILABLE TO YOU AT THE TIME OF YOUR MISTAKE

Memory Is A Gift. Use it.

Obviously, you made a wrong move. What were the *options* at the time? Could you have done it *differently?* Did you do your very *best?* "For which of you, intending to build a tower, sitteth not down first, and counteth the cost, whether he have *sufficient* to finish it?" (Luke 14:28).

▶ *Sometimes what appears to be a mistake was the only possible decision at the time!* Don't waste valuable time on unavoidable circumstances. Perhaps a mistake wasn't made at all!

▶ By carefully *evaluating* the past, helps you avoid making the *same* mistake again.

Your Future
Is Decided
By Who
You Believe.

-MIKE MURDOCK

≈ 5 ≈

IDENTIFY THE PEOPLE YOU PERMITTED TO INFLUENCE YOU DURING THE TIME OF YOUR MISTAKE

Everybody Listens To Somebody.

A minister friend once told me, "Mike, I missed God's perfect will during ten long years of my life."

"What caused it?" I asked.

"I got overly tired," he said. "I overreacted to criticism from a disgruntled deacon. I just up and resigned my church before God was finished with my ministry there. It was the biggest mistake of my entire life."

Fatigue Distorts Judgment.

Are you watching too much television? Neglecting consistent church attendance? Unhealthy friendships? Your ego? Be honest!

Your dreams and goals can be destroyed by listening to the wrong advice.

Even *sickness* can greatly affect your decision-making.

A frustrated friend may be creating a *climate of discontent* for you. "He that walketh with wise *men* shall be wise: but a companion of fools shall be destroyed" (Proverbs 13:20).

▶ Whose Counsel Do You Treasure Most?

▶ Whose Advice Do You Consistently Ignore?
▶ Whose Success Do You Most Admire?
▶ Whose Wisdom Do You Aggressively Pursue?
▶ Who Are The Top 7 People In Your Circle Of Counsel And Why Have You Chosen Them?

RECOMMENDED BOOKS:
B-14 Seeds Of Wisdom On Relationships (32 pages/$3)

≈ 6 ≈

BE WILLING TO TASTE THE PAIN OF YOUR MISTAKE

Learn From The School Of Pain.

There are times God wants us to feel the *loss* from our wrong choices. In Luke 15, the prodigal son *"came to himself"* when he became hungry. "He would fain have filled his belly with the husks that the swine did eat" (verse 16).

Pain can motivate you. God may allow you to crash! *If He cushioned every blow, you would never grow.*

However, I assure you, your Father will not allow the suffering and aching to become a permanent feeling. He will use it to develop a *humility,* a *compassion* for others and a *reminder* of why Jesus Christ died on Calvary for the sins of the world: "But He knoweth the way that I take: *when* He hath tried me, I shall come forth as gold" (Job 23:10).

The Psalmist said: "It is good for me that I have been afflicted; that I might learn Thy statutes" (Psalm 119:71).

Hebrews 5:8 says: "Though He were a Son, yet learned He obedience by the things which He suffered."

The Quickest Cure For Ingratitude Is Loss. Don't leave the scene of pain too quickly. The exposure to pain can create a worthy memory...that protects you for years later.

Those who learn from the pain will succeed beyond their dreams.

All Men Fall...
The Great Ones
Get Back Up.

-MIKE MURDOCK

∿ 7 ∿

IDENTIFY THE WISDOM YOU HAVE EXTRACTED FROM YOUR MISTAKE

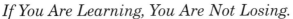

If You Are Learning, You Are Not Losing.

Take a sheet of paper. List lessons learned. "...write the vision, and make it plain" (Habakkuk 2:2). Ask yourself these questions.

▶ What *weaknesses in myself* does this mistake reveal?

▶ What have I learned about *others* during this time?

▶ What do the *Scriptures* teach in regard to my mistake?

Take time to *think* and to *hear* with your *heart* what you can understand through this time of learning. Study the lives of people who made the *same* mistake and *recovered*. Focus on what you can do *now*.

Document secrets learned in your Personal Wisdom Journal.

RECOMMENDED BOOKS AND TAPES:
TS-03 How To Walk Through Fire (6 tapes/$30)
TS-40 Wisdom For Crisis Times (6 tapes/$30)
B-40   Wisdom For Crisis Times (252 pages/$9)

Never Discuss
Your Problem
With Someone Incapable
Of Solving It.

-MIKE MURDOCK

～ 8 ～

STOP DISCUSSING YOUR MISTAKE WITH THOSE YOU WANT TO FORGET IT

Silence Cannot Be Misquoted.

A few choice friends will gladly lend an ear as you release your pent-up hurt. You may need it...with the *right* people. However, it is even more effective to discuss it with *God.* "In the day when I cried Thou answeredst me, and strengthenedst me *with* strength in my soul" (Psalm 138:3). "I sought the Lord, and He heard me, and delivered me from all my fears" (Psalm 34:4).

1. Stop Displaying Your Weaknesses Unnecessarily. It *magnifies* your mistakes. It becomes ammunition in the hands of your enemies. "I am *learning*, not losing." Talk to yourself. "He that hath knowledge spareth his words...Give instruction to a wise man, and he will be yet wiser: teach a just man, and he will increase in learning" (Proverbs 17:27; 9:9).

2. Be Gentle But Firm In Refusing Others The Liberty To Focus On Your Past Failures. "Brethren, I count not myself to have apprehended: but this one thing I do, forgetting those things which are behind...I press toward the mark for the prize of the high calling of God in Christ Jesus" (Philippians 3:13,14).

3.   Memorize The Scriptural Solution.
"Remember ye not the former things, neither consider the things of old. Behold, I will do a new thing; now it shall spring forth; shall ye not know it? I will even make a way in the wilderness, and rivers in the desert" (Isaiah 43:18,19).

4.   Empty Your Energy Into Your *Future*. Visualize The *Future* You Desire, *Not* The Past You Despise.

Anything fed...grows.

RECOMMENDED BOOKS AND TAPES:
TS-25 Secrets Of The Richest Man Who Ever Lived (6 tapes/$30)
B-99 Secrets Of The Richest Man Who Ever Lived (177 pages/$10)

≈ 9 ≈

MOVE SWIFTLY TO MAKE RESTITUTION WITH ANYONE YOU HAVE WRONGED

The Proof Of Repentance Is Restitution.

True repentance involves *restitution*—mending broken fences. One definition of restitution is "the *final restoration* of all things and persons into harmony with God's will."

Restitution is a faith-releasing principle that purifies your conscience. It unties the hands of God to work freely in your behalf. "If a man shall steal an ox, or a sheep, and kill it, or sell it; he shall restore five oxen for an ox, and four sheep for a sheep" (Exodus 22:1). "And Zacchaeus stood, and said unto the Lord; Behold, Lord, the half of my goods I give to the poor; and if I have taken any thing from any man by false accusation, I restore *him* fourfold" (Luke 19:8).

Several years ago, a man was having severe marital problems, stomach pains and could not sleep at night. He broke down and confessed to me that he had embezzled money from his company.

"You must make it right," I insisted. "Go to your president and totally level with him. Admit your mistake."

Though he feared losing his job, the man truly recognized the value of restitution. Guess what happened? *Not only was he permitted to keep his job, but later received a promotion from the president who respected his openness and new convictions!*

Pain is often a passage to a miracle.

My dear friend, Robb Thompson, often shares the miracle testimony following his conversion to Christ. Those who saw the *proof* of his changed heart were forever affected by his willingness to *correct* the wrongs.

✎ 10 ✎

ALLOW A SEASON OF TIME FOR YOUR RECOVERY

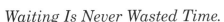

Waiting Is Never Wasted Time.

Time is the Bridge between Seed and Harvest. It is natural to want an *instant* change in your circumstances. Take for instance, the emotional cycle following a divorce, often creates loneliness, anger, guilt, bitterness, frustration, emptiness, depression and past memories. How do you cope with it? It isn't always as easy as glib-tongued friends may try to make it appear.

Healing takes time.

Of course, there are things you can do to *hasten* the healing, just as it is possible to *slow* your healing process. The wisest man who ever lived said: "To every thing there is a season, and a time," (Ecclesiastes 3:1).

But do not weary of waiting for your complete miracle. Give yourself space: "And let us not be weary in well doing: for in due season we shall reap, if we faint not" (Galatians 6:9).

Meanwhile, during "Recovery Zone," *learn* all you can, cultivate *compassion,* exercise *faith* and develop control in all areas of your life.

Time matters.

Waiting is rarely a waste.

The Willingness To Wait Is The Proof Of Trust.

What You Make Happen
For Others
God Will Make Happen
For You.

-MIKE MURDOCK

❧ 11 ❧

FOCUS ON HELPING SOMEONE ELSE ACHIEVE THEIR GOALS

Somebody Is Waiting For You.

Jesus Christ was our Master Example of concentrating on the success of *others*. He was a Success-Maker. He reprogrammed the mentality of losers and made them winners.

Jesus Cared About Others

He took the time:

▶ To compliment (Matthew 8:10)

▶ To heal the sick (Matthew 8:16)

▶ To forgive sin (Matthew 9:2)

▶ To advise ministers (Matthew 10:1-42)

▶ To teach the unlearned (Matthew 5-7)

▶ To expose frauds (Matthew 23)

He created *success situations* for people.

Look around you! What can you do now to be a more effective employee on your job? A loving husband or wife? A more helpful friend?

1.   "Withhold not good from them to whom it is due, when it is in the power of thine hand to do it" (Proverbs 3:27).

2.   "Render therefore to all their dues: tribute to whom tribute is dues: custom to whom custom: fear to whom fear: honour to whom honour" (Romans 13:7).

3.   "Knowing that whatsoever good thing any

man doeth, the same shall he receive of the Lord, whether he be bond or free" (Ephesians 6:8).

Never forget the greatest Wisdom Principle in scriptural success: "What You Make Happen For Others, God Will Make Happen For You!" (see Ephesians 6:8).

You Are The Miracle Someone Is Waiting For.

❧ 12 ❧

DEVELOP THE MENTALITY OF A WINNER

You Become What You Think.

So, start hanging "Success Photographs" on the walls of your own mind!

▶ *Picture Health.*

▶ *Picture Prosperity.*

▶ *Picture a Happy Marriage.*

▶ *Picture Overcoming.*

▶ *Picture Power.*

When You Control Your Thoughts, You Control Your Life: "Whatsoever things are true...honest...just...pure...lovely...of good report; if there be any virtue, and if there be any praise, think on these things" (Philippians 4:8).

Visualize What You Want To Materialize!

Some time ago I bought a car. With it, I received an owner's handbook on how to operate it and solve possible problems. It was to help me enjoy driving my new car, and avoid some frustrating situations.

God, the Creator, provided the same service to you and me to enjoy living in His world. His Success Handbook is the Bible. It is your source for How To Live On Planet Earth. Without it, you may easily sabotage your life.

Read the Bible daily. It will place positive and powerful mind-photographs in your thinking. You will begin to understand God, others and yourself in a beautiful new light!

Say...what God is *seeing*.

Speak...your expectations, *not* your experiences.

RECOMMENDED BOOKS AND TAPES:
B-49 The Proverbs 31 Woman (67 pages/$7)
B-80 The Greatest Success Habit On Earth (32 pages/$5)
B-99 Secrets Of The Richest Man Who Ever Lived (177 pages/$10)
TS-25 Secrets Of The Richest Man Who Ever Lived (6 tapes/$30)

❧ 13 ❧

PRACTICE A CELEBRATION ROUTINE AFTER EVERY PERSONAL ACHIEVEMENT

Learn The Art Of Celebration.

Greatness Is Turning Pebble Moments Into Memory Mountains.

Learn the art.

When you find a parking space exactly where you wanted...a dress you wanted, on sale for one-half price...a gasoline station open when your tank shows empty—*talk about it!* Immediately verbalize a big, *"Thanks, Father!"* Tell your friends!

Appreciate tiny blessings!

Cultivate the "Attitude of Gratitude!"

Look for *the good* in others.

Look for *the good* in *yourself!*

Recognize your own accomplishments, no matter how insignificant they may appear. Jesus told a great truth in Matthew 25 about the Principle of Recognition and Rewards: "...thou has been faithful over a few things, I will make thee ruler over many things:" (verses 21,23).

Express thanksgiving for the little blessings. Greater blessings will follow.

Gratitude Creates Joy.

Joy Births Praise.

Praise Decides Divine Presence.

Divine Presence Creates Change.

The Greatest Quality
On Earth
Is The Willingness
To Become.

-MIKE MURDOCK

✐ 14 ✐

START YOUR COMEBACK NOW

You Are Closer To A Miracle Than You Have Ever Been.

Begin today. God linked you to this Wisdom Book! God is a *now* God. He wants you to become a WINNER...today! Pray this Prayer aloud now:

"Holy Spirit, I *need* You. I *want* You. Forgive me for every mistake I have made with my life. I accept Jesus Christ as the Lord and Master of my life and receive Your forgiveness. Fill my heart and life with Your peace and joy. I place all my *memories* of yesterday's mistakes at the Cross of Calvary. Send the right people into my life this week to help me develop and grow into a powerful champion for You. In Jesus' name. Amen."

Write me today! Tell me how this book helped you and ask for your gift copy of "31 Keys To A New Beginning." I know our new friendship will unlock the Miracle of your next Season!

DECISION

Will You Accept Jesus As Your Personal Savior Today?

The Bible says, "That if thou shalt confess with thy mouth the Lord Jesus, and shalt believe in thine heart that God hath raised Him from the dead, thou shalt be saved" (Romans 10:9).

Pray this prayer from your heart today!

"Dear Jesus, I believe that You died for me and rose again on the third day. I confess I am a sinner...I need Your love and forgiveness...Come into my heart. Forgive my sins. I receive Your eternal life. Confirm Your love by giving me peace, joy and supernatural love for others. Amen."

DR. MIKE MURDOCK

is in tremendous demand as one of the most dynamic speakers in America today.

More than 14,000 audiences in 38 countries have attended his meetings and seminars. Hundreds of invitations come to him from churches, colleges and business corporations. He is a noted author of over 140 books, including the best sellers, *"The Leadership Secrets of Jesus"* and *"Secrets of the Richest Man Who Ever Lived."* Thousands view his weekly television program, *"Wisdom Keys with Mike Murdock."* Many attend his Schools of Wisdom that he hosts in many cities of America.

Clip and Mail

☐ Yes, Mike! I made a decision to accept Christ as my personal Savior today. Please send me my free gift of your book, *"31 Keys to a New Beginning"* to help me with my new life in Christ. *(B-48)*

NAME _____ BIRTHDAY _____

ADDRESS _____

CITY _____ STATE _____ ZIP _____

PHONE _____ E-MAIL _____

Mail form to:
The Wisdom Center · 4051 Denton Hwy. · Ft. Worth, TX 76117
1-888-WISDOM-1 (1-888-947-3661) · Website: **thewisdomcenter.tv**

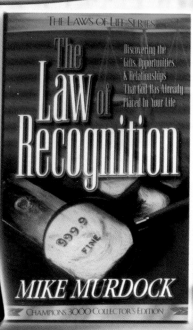

UNCOMMON WISDOM FOR UNCOMMON POWER

THE *Power* 7

The Power 7 Pak

- ► Seeds of Wisdom on The Secret Place (B-115 / $5)
- ► Seeds of Wisdom on The Holy Spirit (B-116 / $5)
- ► Seeds of Wisdom on Your Assignment (B-122 / $5)
- ► Seeds of Wisdom on Goal Setting (B-127 / $5)
- ► My Personal Dream Book (B-143 / $5)
- ► 101 Wisdom Keys (B-45 / $5)
- ► 31 Keys To A New Beginning (B-48 / $5)

The Wisdom Center

All 7 Books
Only $20
WBL-19

Wisdom Is The Principal Thing

Add 10% For S/H

B **THE WISDOM CENTER** **1-888-WISDOM1**   — Website: —
4051 Denton Highway ¥ Fort Worth, TX 76117   **(1-888-947-3661)**   THEWISDOMCENTER.TV

Financial Success.

- ▶ 8 Scriptural Reasons You Should Pursue Financial Prosperity

- ▶ The Secret Prayer Key You Need When Making A Financial Request To God

- ▶ The Weapon Of Expectation And The 5 Miracles It Unlocks

- ▶ How To Discern Those Who Qualify To Receive Your Financial Assistance

- ▶ How To Predict The Miracle Moment God Will Schedule Your Financial Breakthrough

- ▶ Habits Of Uncommon Achievers

- ▶ The Greatest Success Law I Ever Discovered

- ▶ How To Discern Your Place Of Assignment, The Only Place Financial Provision Is Guaranteed

- ▶ 3 Secret Keys In Solving Problems For Others

The Wisdom Center

Video Pak
AMVIDEO | **$30**
Buy 1-Get 1 Free
(A $60 Value!)

Wisdom Is The Principal Thing

Add 10% For S/H

Songs From The Secret Place

The Music Ministry of MIKE MURDOCK

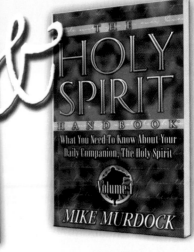

Love Songs To The Holy Spirit
Birthed In The Secret Place

THE HOLY SPIRIT HANDBOOK
What You Need To Know About Your Daily Companion, The Holy Spirit
Volume 1
MIKE MURDOCK

The Wisdom Center

6 Tapes | $30

PAK-007

Wisdom Is The Principal Thing

Free Book
B-100 ($10 Value)
ENCLOSED!

Wisdom Is The Principal Thing

Songs...

1. A Holy Place
2. Anything You Want
3. Everything Comes From You
4. Fill This Place With Your Presence
5. First Thing Every Morning
6. Holy Spirit, I Want To Hear You
7. Holy Spirit, Move Again
8. Holy Spirit, You Are Enough
9. I Don't Know What I Would Do Without You
10. I Let Go (Of Anything That Stops Me)
11. I'll Just Fall On You
12. I Love You, Holy Spirit
13. I'm Building My Life Around You
14. I'm Giving Myself To You
15. I'm In Love! I'm In Love!
16. I Need Water (Holy Spirit, You're My Well)
17. In The Secret Place
18. In Your Presence, I'm Always Changed
19. In Your Presence (Miracles Are Born)
20. I've Got To Live In Your Presence
21. I Want To Hear Your Voice
22. I Will Do Things Your Way
23. Just One Day At A Time
24. Meet Me In The Secret Place
25. More Than Ever Before
26. Nobody Else Does What You Do
27. No No Walls!
28. Nothing Else Matters Anymore (Since I've Been In The Presence Of You Lord)
29. Nowhere Else
30. Once Again You've Answered
31. Only A Fool Would Try (To Live Without You)
32. Take Me Now
33. Teach Me How To Please You
34. There's No Place I'd Rather Be
35. Thy Word Is All That Matters
36. When I Get In Your Presence
37. You're The Best Thing (That's Ever Happened To Me)
38. You Are Wonderful!
39. You've Done It Once
40. You Keep Changing Me
41. You Satisfy

Add 10% For S/H

D **THE WISDOM CENTER**
4051 Denton Highway ¥ Fort Worth, TX 76117

1-888-WISDOM1
(1-888-947-3661)

Website:
THEWISDOMCENTER.TV

The Uncommon Woman

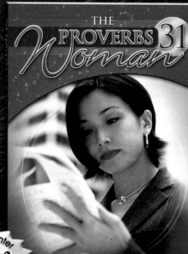

- ▸ **Master Keys In Understanding The Man In Your Life**
- ▸ **The One Thing Every Man Attempts To Move Away From**
- ▸ **The Dominant Difference Between A Wrong Woman And A Right Woman**
- ▸ **What Causes Men To Withdraw**

MIKE MURDOCK

THE WISDOM FOR WOMEN SERIES

THIRTY - ONE SECRETS of an UNFORGETTABLE WOMAN

Master Secrets from the Life of Ruth

THE WISDOM CENTER
MIKE MURDOCK•P.O. Box 99• Denton, Texas

31 Secrets of an Unforgettable Woman

The Wisdom Center
6 Tapes **$30**
PAK-009
Wisdom Is The Principal Thing

Free Book Enclosed!
Wisdom Is The Principal Thing

 THE WISDOM CENTER
4051 Denton Highway ¥ Fort Worth, TX 76117

1-888-WISDOM1
(1-888-947-3661)

Website:
THEWISDOMCENTER.TV

E

UNCOMMON WISDOM FOR AN UNCOMMON MINISTRY

FOR Ministers ONLY

THE UNCOMMON MINISTER — Power Principles For Hitting Your Target For Success In Ministry — 1 — MIKE MURDOCK

THE UNCOMMON MINISTER — Wisdom Keys For A Ministry Of Excellence And Greatness — 2

THE UNCOMMON MINISTER — Winning Principles For Achieving Greatness In Your Ministry — 3

THE UNCOMMON MINISTER — Principles On The Path To A Victorious Ministry — 4 — MURDOCK

THE UNCOMMON MINISTER — Sign Posts On The Road To Excellence In Ministry — 5 — MIKE MURDOCK

THE UNCOMMON MINISTER — Powerful Steps To A More Powerful Ministry — 6 — MIKE MURDOCK

THE UNCOMMON MINISTER — Steps To Achieving Your Goals In Your Ministry — 7 — MIKE MURDOCK

Volume 1 E
Volume 2 E
Volume 3 E
Volume 4 B
Volume 5 B
Volume 6 E
Volume 7 E

When God wants to touch a nation, He raises up a preacher. It is Uncommon Men and Women of God who have driven back the darkness and shielded the unlearned and rebellious from devastation by satanic forces. They offer the breath of life to a dead world. They open Golden Doors to Change. They unleash Forces of Truth in an age of deception.

An Uncommon Minister is prepared through seasons of pain, encounters with God, a mentors. Having sat at the feet of Uncommon Mentors his entire life, Dr. Mike Murdock shar practical but personal keys to increase the excellence and productivity of your ministry. Ea volume of "The Uncommon Minister" is handy, convenient and easy to read. Your load will lighter, your journey happier, and your effectiveness increased in "doing the will of the Father.

 THE WISDOM CENTER **1-888-WISDOM1** Website:
4051 Denton Highway ¥ Fort Worth, TX 76117 **(1-888-947-3661)** THEWISDOMCENTER.TV

F

What Every Parent Has Been Waiting For...

A 12-Month Family Mentorship Program.
Over 365 Chapters Of Wisdom For Every Day Of The Year.

- 31 Keys To A
  New Beginning
- 31 Facts About Wisdom
- 31 Secrets of an
  Unforgettable Woman
- The Holy Spirit
  Handbook
- The Assignment:
  Volumes 1-4

- 31 Reasons People
  Do Not Receive
  Their Financial Harvest
- Secrets of The Richest
  Man Who Ever Lived
- The 3 Most Important
  Things In Your Life
- 31 Secrets To
  Career Success

The Wisdom Center

Only $89

WBL-16 / $120 Value

Wisdom Is The Principal Thing

Add 10% For S/H

 **THE WISDOM CENTER**
4051 Denton Highway ¥ Fort Worth, TX 76117

1-888-WISDOM1
(1-888-947-3661)

Website:
THEWISDOMCENTER.TV

G

GIFTS OF WISDOM....

FOR *Mothers* ONLY!

*Each Book Sold Separately

- **One-Minute Pocket Bible for Mothers** (B-52 / $5)

- **The Gift of Wisdom for Mothers** (B-70 / $10)

- **The Mother's Topical Bible** (B-36 / $10)

- **The Proverbs 31 Woman** (B-49 / $7)

- **The Uncommon Mother** (B-132 / $10)

- **Thirty-One Secrets of an Unforgettable Woman** (B-57 / $9)

The Wisdom Center

**WISDOM...
The Greatest
Gift Of All!**

Wisdom Is The Principal Thing

THE WISDOM CENTER   1-888-WISDOM1
4051 Denton Highway ¥ Fort Worth, TX 76117   (1-888-947-3661)

Website:
THEWISDOMCENTER.TV   1

GIFTS OF WISDOM...

SPECIALTY *Bibles*

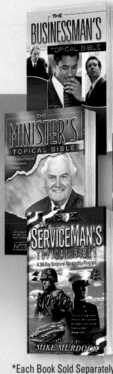
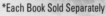

*Each Book Sold Separately

My Gift Of Appreciation...
The Wisdom Commentary

The Wisdom Commentary includes
52 topics...for mentoring your
family every week of the year.

These topics include:

- Abilities
- Achievement
- Anointing
- Assignment
- Bitterness
- Blessing
- Career
- Change
- Children
- Dating
- Depression
- Discipline
- Divorce
- Dreams And Goals
- Enemy
- Enthusiasm
- Favor
- Finances
- Fools

- Giving
- Goal-Setting
- God
- Happiness
- Holy Spirit
- Ideas
- Intercession
- Jobs
- Loneliness
- Love
- Mentorship
- Ministers
- Miracles
- Mistakes
- Money
- Negotiation
- Prayer
- Problem-Solving
- Protégés

- Satan
- Secret Place
- Seed-Faith
- Self-Confidence
- Struggle
- Success
- Time-Management
- Understanding
- Victory
- Weaknesses
- Wisdom
- Word Of God
- Words
- Work

Gift Of Appreciation
For Your
Sponsorship
Seed of $100
or More
Gift Of Appreciation

My Gift Of Appreciation To My Sponsors!
Those Who Sponsor One Square Foot In
The Completion Of The Wisdom Center!

Thank you so much for becoming a part of this wonderful project...The completion of The Wisdom Center!
The total purchase and renovation cost of this facility (10,000 square feet) is just over $1,000,000. This is
approximately $100 per square foot. **The Wisdom Commentary is my Gift of Appreciation for your
sponsorship Seed of $100...that sponsors one square foot of The Wisdom Center. Become a Sponsor!**
You will love this Volume 1, of The Wisdom Commentary. It is my exclusive Gift of Appreciation for The
Wisdom Key Family who partners with me in the Work of God as a Sponsor.

Add 10% For S/H

 THE WISDOM CENTER 4051 Denton Highway • Fort Worth, TX 76117 **1-888-WISDOM1** **(1-888-947-3661)** Website: THEWISDOMCENTER.TV **K**

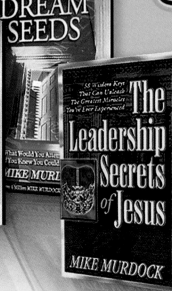
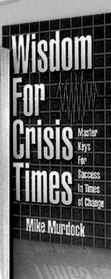

The Wisdom Journal

Wisdom Journal • Wisdom Jou

"Write The Things Which Thou Hast Seen, And The Things Which Are, And The Things Which Shall Be Hereafter."

-Revelation 1:19

Stunningly beautiful deep Black and Gold Leatherette. Contains 160 pages for your personal journalizing and diary...a different Wisdom Key for each day...it also includes:

- ► 101 Wisdom Keys
- ► 31 Facts About Favor
- ► 31 Facts About Wisdom
- ► 31 Facts About The Holy Spirit
- ► 31 Qualities Of An Unforgettable Woman
- ► 58 Leadership Secrets Of Jesus
- ► Read The Bible Through In A Year Program
- ► Sample Page For Effective Note Taking

My Wisdom Journal

The Wisdom Center

$20 Each

B-163

Wisdom Is The Principal Thing

Add 10% For S/H

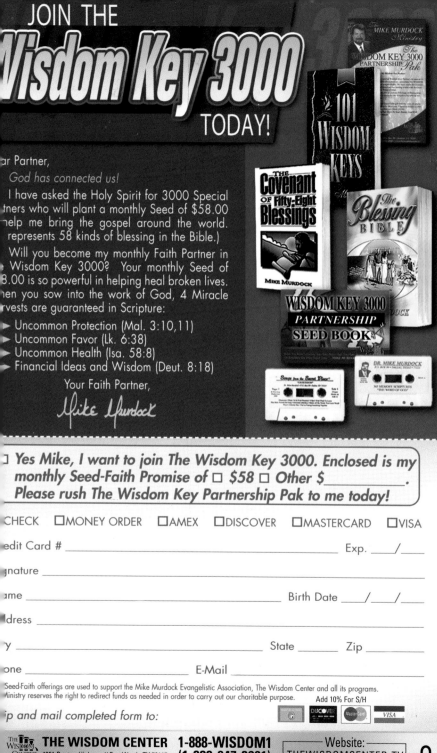

JOIN THE
Wisdom Key 3000
TODAY!

ar Partner,

God has connected us!

I have asked the Holy Spirit for 3000 Special
tners who will plant a monthly Seed of $58.00
elp me bring the gospel around the world.
represents 58 kinds of blessing in the Bible.)

Will you become my monthly Faith Partner in
Wisdom Key 3000? Your monthly Seed of
8.00 is so powerful in helping heal broken lives.
en you sow into the work of God, 4 Miracle
vests are guaranteed in Scripture:

► Uncommon Protection (Mal. 3:10,11)
► Uncommon Favor (Lk. 6:38)
► Uncommon Health (Isa. 58:8)
► Financial Ideas and Wisdom (Deut. 8:18)

Your Faith Partner,

Mike Murdock

❑ **Yes Mike, I want to join The Wisdom Key 3000. Enclosed is my
monthly Seed-Faith Promise of ❑ $58 ❑ Other $_____.
Please rush The Wisdom Key Partnership Pak to me today!**

CHECK ❑MONEY ORDER ❑AMEX ❑DISCOVER ❑MASTERCARD ❑VISA

edit Card # _____ Exp. ___/___

gnature _____

ame _____ Birth Date ___/___/___

dress _____

y _____ State _____ Zip _____

one _____ E-Mail _____

Seed-Faith offerings are used to support the Mike Murdock Evangelistic Association, The Wisdom Center and all its programs.
inistry reserves the right to redirect funds as needed in order to carry out our charitable purpose. Add 10% For S/H

p and mail completed form to:

THE WISDOM CENTER 1-888-WISDOM1
4051 Denton Highway ¥ Fort Worth, TX 76117 (1-888-947-3661)

Website:
THEWISDOMCENTER.TV 0